AF421698

CONFESSIONS OF A
FUNCTIONING ~~ALCOHOLIC~~ MOTHER

CONFESSIONS OF A
FUNCTIONING ~~ALCOHOLIC~~ MOTHER

MEGAN DELZELL

INTRO

I spent hours struggling to organize these writings to find some sort of flow. Something that would show the progression of trauma, grief, thought, and growth.

I realized none of these things are linear. I was trying to format them in a storyline as if each happened on its own when it isn't often that these things happen independently of one another. Each thing that happens in our life overlaps the other, and usually, our growth coincides with a current trauma or addiction. We are always learning. Growth happens even in the darkest of places.

This book is a collection of writings from moments in my life. It chronicles a decades-long grief process after losing my father at 21 to alcohol. I discuss my abusive relationships, losing a child, having children, addiction, sobriety, mental illness, and everything in between.

These poems may not have a linear flow of love and loss, but then again, when does life?

– MEGAN DELZELL

MY LIFE

GRACE	1
MEMORIES (MY FATHER IS)	3
TOO MUCH	5
BAY	9
DAD'S BOTTLE	12
THE DAY I CHOSE	14
MEMORY LOOP	16
LETTERS	18
I MISSED YOU TODAY	19
GRIEF'S BIRTHDAY	22
BRAKES	26
DOORWAY	28
3 WORDS	30
CLAY	32
INSANITY	34
MY FATHER'S MOTHER	38
SETTING YOU FREE	40
ONCE UPON A TIME	42
DOT DOT DOT	44
HOLE IN THE GROUND	45
SILENCE	50
MOM	52
FATHERS	54
FOREVER	56
RETROSPECTION	58
PAIGE	60
ONE PLUS ONE	64
THE NIGHT WE SAID GOODBYE	66
18	68
GRANNY'S SHOES	70
PINK CLOUD	72
POSTPARTUM	74
4TH OF JULY	77
TODAYS NEWS	80
HOMELESS	82
SADNESS	84
ALBUQUERQUE	86
NARCISSUS	90
CLOSURE	94
IMPOSTER	96
SWEET BOY	100
LAST BABY	102
LITTLE HANDS	104
I DON'T LIVE THERE ANYMORE	106

GRACE

If I could name one thing that has made sobriety possible, it is forgiveness. It's about having grace, and giving it to others too.

Before sobriety, I could never forgive those who had wronged me. If there was a medal for holding a grudge, I'd win gold every time. As I progressed through sobriety, I began to question myself. Am I holding them to a standard higher than I hold myself to? How many people have I wronged throughout my life? How often have I wished that forgiveness was bestowed upon me? Yet here I stand, judging the people who have wronged me, expecting them to turn around and apologize, most of them probably don't even know that they've done anything wrong.

In my addiction fueled need to be right, I didn't think to account for their childhood, their past traumas, or the lack of tools (or the want) to improve themselves. It led me to an optimistic belief: Everyone that I've encountered is trying with whatever tools they have in their emotional toolbox. Some have the tools to make themselves better, and some don't even know the tools exist.

From this epiphany, I came to understand that people often times don't even realize that they're hurting others, all they're doing is continuing what they were taught . I was always taught that being a good person is the key to life, and that you should always treat others the way you want to be treated. I never stopped to think that some people might have been taught that violence is the way to communicate, or that emotions mean you're weak. These people's way of communicating or emotionally surviving can be off-putting, offensive, hurtful, without even realizing it. How can I expect these people to seek tools for a problem they don't even know exists? How often do these people not even realize there are tools available?

I believe this is where Grace comes in. People are flawed, whether it's massively or minimally, everyone has a flaw. That old phrase "you can't please everyone" shows that if I am not capable of pleasing everybody in the world, then I am flawed to someone. If no one is perfect, and everyone is flawed in some capacity, then we are all similar, just speaking different emotional languages.

By accepting imperfection, I have removed the expectation of perfection, and that opens me up to forgiveness. How much easier is it to forgive someone you know is not perfect? I easily forgive a child for spilling food on themselves, because I know they haven't learned how to do it properly. Why don't I forgive someone who has not learned how to exist on a higher plane?

Why do I forgive my child for an emotional outburst, knowing they do not have the capacity for higher emotional intelligence yet, but I somehow expect all adults to have achieve emotional intelligence? Do we graduate from emotional intelligence college? Do they hand out degrees? Who is actually running the emotional intelligence IQ department?

Putting it in terms like that makes it seem foolish. None of us get a course in emotional intelligence. None of us are taught based off a nation wide rubric how to deal with tough situations. We learn these things from our parents, from our peers, siblings, family members. Well, what happens when those people didn't graduate at the top of their class in the emotional intelligence college? We end up with people who have no idea how to communicate, problem solve, interact, or deal with emotions.

Welcome to addiction.

MEMORIES

My Father was Herbal Essence shampoo and a pony tail.
He was an hour long wait to get into the bathroom
and a collection of reader's digest.
He was a yellow Gatorade and a beat up old truck, a tool box
and a bent checkbook.
He was an ashtray full of coins and a truck that smelled like
sawdust.
My Father was jean shorts and a white T Shirt, work boots and
big white socks.
He was steamed peas, steak and spaghetti.
He was a smile with scrunched eyes and red cheeks, a sunburn
and a goatee.
He was a laugh with a wheeze, he was a Terry Lumber T Shirt.
He was My Littlest Pet Shop for Christmas and a bunny
for Easter.
He was guinea pigs and a flag lot, he was the beach and ZZ Top.
He was a Lakers game and Stevie Nicks.
He was a dirt bike and Rollerblades, a Golden Retriever
and hardwood floors.
My dad was camping and fishing, a little tin can boat
and bare feet.
He was learning to drive a stick, a big hill, and a drivers license.
He was high school graduation and horseback riding lessons.
He was avocados and a rock collection, an engine and a
hummingbird in the dryer.
He was Scotland and baby diapers, aftershock and limes.
He was cat scratch fever and brushing my teeth.
He was the "turn the channel" about the monster under the bed.
He was "Don't" when you poked his belly button, he was Vern.
He was Grandpa and tears, he was a back massager in the
delivery room.
He was I'm proud of you, and Rise above it.
He was tears and don't leave, he was tears and come home.
He was tears and come see me, he was a sudden phone call.

He was laughter and happiness, he was sanity and glue.
He was the best man to ever walk this earth.
He was the glue that held the family together, he was the family
that never got included.
He was sadness and pain, he was strength and fight.
He was an alcoholic, who lost his battle with the bottle at 48.
My father was an amazing man, but alcohol stole him and
left random fond memories where he used to stand.

TOO MUCH

For most of my life, I have been the black sheep. I've always been told I was "too much." Too much noise, too much energy, too many ideas, too much indecision, too much of everything. I always felt the need to dial myself back, since me at full volume was more than most could handle.

Not being accepted for being fully myself led to me feeling removed. I remember as a child regularly being angry with myself for being "too much" and asking why I couldn't just be normal so family members would love me as much as they did the ones who weren't too much.

My mind only works at 100mph. It always has. It's like my dad's old truck where you'd pump the gas a couple of times before dropping the choke and it would roar to life, pinning the RPMs in the red, fan belt screaming.

I know I'm too much. I'm always processing the next thought in a conversation, anticipating the participants' responses in some internal morbid chess game, where the more I do, the better I'll be at being less. I guess it stems from a need for perfection. If I can guess their response, I can say the perfect thing to make them like me, I can come up with the perfect quip to make them laugh. The harder I work, the more I am "too much", the better I can be at not being too much, which will mean acceptance. Understanding. Love.

I've always felt my father was the only one who ever understood me. He never told me I was too much. He enjoyed my internal radio at full volume. He loved the ideas that spewed from my mind like a broken water hose seal.
I don't remember ever feeling the need to dumb myself down,

lower the volume, or quiet my soul around him. I blasted myself at full volume and he loved to sing along.

I often wonder if his radio was just as loud, and perhaps my volume made him feel less alone.

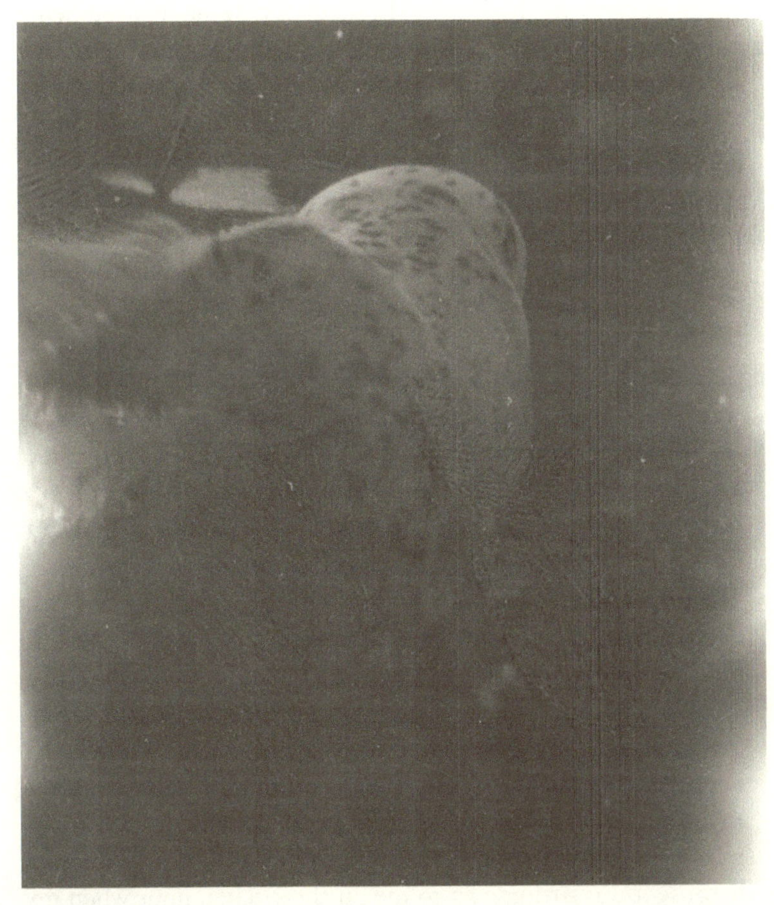

BAY

I knew I should have never let her leave to visit him for those two weeks. I pushed back against the idea of letting her go to visit him, and almost said no. Something inside of me knew it would be the last time I saw her. Something inside of me knew my world was about to end. The alcoholic in me rejoiced being child free for two weeks, but what was left of the mother in me hated her being away from me for even a day. I relented and walked her to the plane, handed her to her father across those gates and told her to be a good girl for daddy. She didn't cry that day and I assured myself he would take good care of her.

The day before her return I spent in the bar. Soaking in the last moments of freedom before she returned home, excited to see her but semi-sad to see my freedom reclaimed by the small child that demanded so much from me. Mostly drunk I made my way home to end my afternoon with a nap, planning to make my way back for the evening's round two. A knock on my door awoke me from my stupor and I stumbled to answer it. "You've been served" is all the man had to say before heading to his car. I opened the paperwork and dropped to my knees, screaming. The man walked back from his car into the front yard and wrote down a number for a lawyer and handed it to me. He asked if he could help me inside. I blamed this man for everything and screamed at him to fuck off and die. The next few hours are blacked out in my mind. Despite all my attempts to recall what happened, for the life of me, there is nothing. I know I called my mom, and the bar friend I had been screwing for a couple months. I know I went to the store to buy a bottle of Jameson, because it was sitting next to me on the kitchen floor when my memory returns.

There I sat on the kitchen floor, knife and Jameson seated next to me. My memory comes to as I am midway through writing a letter to Baylee and Dare apologizing for what I was about to do.

I had already consumed half that bottle of Jameson in the 20 minutes it took for anyone to arrive. I told them to leave, but we knew what was going to happen.

The friend, whose name I can't remember, sat next to me on the floor, until the bottle was gone. I demanded another from the store, and in that lapse of supervision I shoved the knife in my forearm. EMT school taught me where the veins and arteries were. I knew how to do this properly.

Letter halfway complete, virtually illegible penmanship between the alcohol and tears, I realized I couldn't drag the knife downwards until I said all I needed to say to them. Until I left them a reason, a letter filled with enough love to get them through a life without me.

I never finished that letter.

DAD'S BOTTLE

What did she whisper when you put her against your lips?

Did she promise freedom?

Did she promise you happiness?

As you held her close and told her your darkest secrets,

did she soothe your restless soul?

Did her embrace make you forget?

Did you realize what was happening,

As she slowly pulled you inside?

As she gently pushed your head under and gave you once last kiss.

THE DAY I CHOSE

You looked up at me.

Hungry,

Seeking comfort,

Warmth,

To be nestled against your mother.

I removed you from my breast,

Never to feed you again,

And suckled the bottle instead.

That day I chose.

I fed addiction,

Instead of my child.

Today,

I may not feed you from my breast

But I feed your soul.

Today, I choose you.

Over and over again.

I will choose you.

MEMORY LOOP

I hope heaven is a place where you relive your favorite memories
as if you never left.

Maybe time slows down, like those moments you hoped would
never end. Maybe you don't even realize you've left this world,
you just wake up in an odd sense of deja vu where your version of
heaven is laid out in a beautiful memory loop.

I often wonder where my dad went. I always thought I would
forever feel him, but I don't. I heard his spirit the night he died,
but after that it went quiet. There have been moments I know he
has intervened, that he had a hand in a blessing that came, but
I've never heard him like I did the night he died.

I'd like to think he's reliving his favorite memories. Fishing and
playing basketball in Mammoth, cheering me on at a softball
game, bbqing on a Sunday while we watched football, riding his
dirt bike with me on the back, even though my mom said no.
Maybe he's fishing in Alaska with his dad, or working on a
construction project at his moms house. Maybe he's flying in a
little Cessna over the forest like he always told me he wanted to do.

Wherever he is, I just hope those memory loops include me.
Even if I can't have him here, and my heart feels as though it will
burst from the pain of missing him, I just hope in some universe,
in some string of time, he and I are still together. I hope he's
smiling that beautiful smile, laughing that loud hilarious laugh,
I hope I'm breathing in that smell of sawdust and old spice mixed
together. I hope I'm not forgetting what his voice sounds like,
and I hope I'm not taking one of those amazing bear hugs for
granted.

LETTERS

I am but a jumble of letters.

A diagnosis.

Acronyms scribbled on paper,

Never in the right order.

His desk needs to be tidied,

And his writing is atrocious.

Focus.

What was he saying?

Acronyms.

I am but a jumble of letters.

I MISSED YOU TODAY

I missed you today
While walking around
So I sang you a song
I sang it right out loud

I wanted to send it to you
But didn't know how
To deliver it to heaven
Up above the clouds

I tied it to a kite
Wrapped tight with a bow
But I needed it higher
It had so far to go!

So I called to the wind
To help me send it up high
Way up to you
Way up up in the sky

So hard the wind puffed
And away my song flew
But it didn't go high enough
It didn't reach you

So I called to the bird
To help me send it up high
Way up to you
Way up up in the sky

The bird carried my gift
And he whistled along
The love note I wrote you
In the form of a song

The bird flew way up up
The farthest he could fly
And he pushed and he pushed
Higher in the sky

The bird slowed down
He could not go any higher
He breathed so heavy
His wings were so tired

So I called to the clouds
To help send up my song
Way up up in the sky
To where you had gone

The clouds carried it high
Further than I could see
So I folded my hands
And I dropped to my knees

Please, Lord, I began
Please help carry my song
Please deliver it way up
Send it where it belongs

I miss them today,
And I want them to know
That they are so loved
So much more than I can show

All I can do is sing a song
And send it up high
Way up up up
To their place in the sky

Right next to you, Lord
Where they belong
So you can listen too
To my little love song

The clouds came back down
And whispered to the bird
Then the bird to wind
Who repeated what he heard

My love note had reached you!
He said you sang right along
You and the Lord
Singing my song

I think I can hear you
From way up on high
The wind carries your tune
Down here from the sky

When I miss you most
I'll send up a song
And I'll listen carefully
To hear you singing along.

GRIEF'S BIRTHDAY

My grief can drive this year.

The hole in my chest is a sophomore in high school.

My sadness is a C student.

My guilt listens to music in a Charger, seats down,

smoke rolling out the windows.

My gut wrenching heartache is shaving.

My memories are a JV basketball star.

The time he's been gone

Is long enough to grow another person.

My grief is 16.

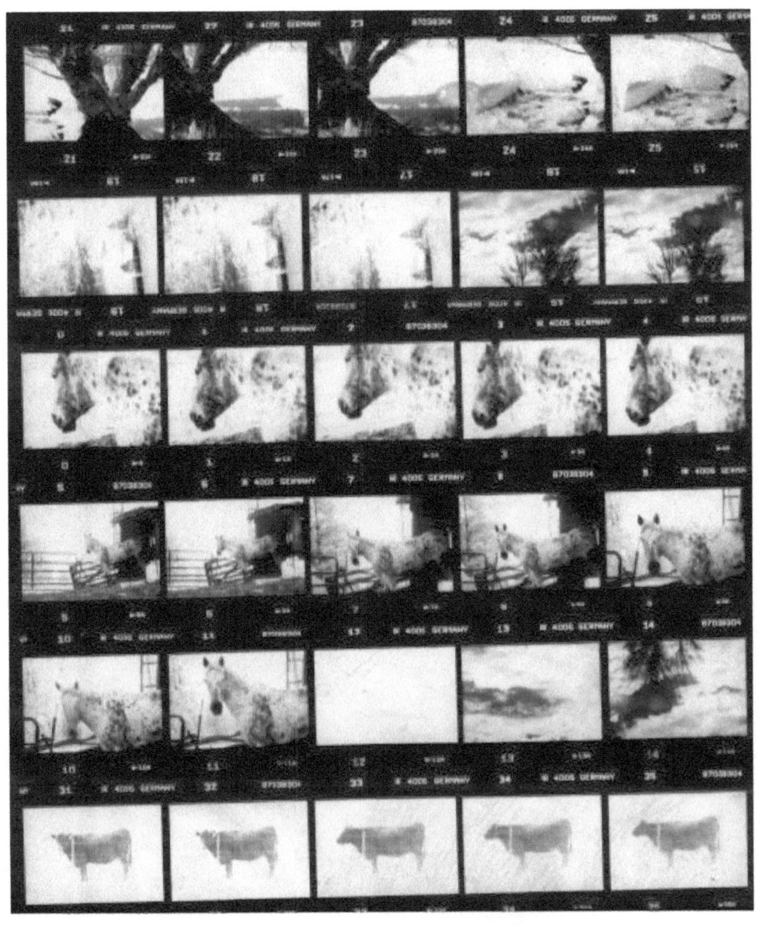

BRAKES

100mph, hitting the e-brake on the curves.
That was me. Driving like a madman towards death, but
somehow avoiding jumping the guard rails by throwing the
e-brake every now and then, only to throttle forward.

My priorities were all about me. Every statement I ever made in
defense of myself started with I. I need this, I deserve that, me,
me, me. My sense of self was all that I could focus on. I only get
one life, why can't I live it to its fullest? Why couldn't I get as
much out of it as I could?

My mind never wandered beyond me. My children came
second, because they have their own life to live, I only have
mine. What kind of mother thinks this?

Alcohol and drugs fed my selfishness, cradled my ego and
whispered how much I was right. Like a demon that crawled
into my throat while I was sleeping, it wrapped it's arms around
my insides and whispered sweet nothings into my ear. I was
consumed, entranced. I was fully under its spell.

Somehow, the Lord granted me a moment of clarity. Like In
a movie, the clouds parted, silence fell. It was gone. My body
cleansed. But a warning was issued, those who have been
possessed will always subconsciously call the demon back. Only
those who stay light on the gas pedal and hold their wheel tight
will avoid that jump over the guard rail.

DOORWAY

I pull the cord on the overhead light, illuminating the small
circle where I stand.

The walls are lined with records and lyrics, the soundtrack
of my life.

Boxes are stacked, gathering cobwebs, full of memories and
demons. Half completed projects lean against each other,
forgotten ambitions. My fingers trace the box lids, torn and bent
from years of opening and closing, stacking and organizing.

The handwriting on each showing the progression of age, titling
contents of years of collections.

Mixed together are happiness and sorrow, toys and heartache.
Adult and child are intertwined, no clear break from when the
two combined.

There are boxes that I open regularly, inhaling innocence.
Little trinkets, a marble and a rock. A pair of shoes, a baseball
mitt, mismatched earrings turning green with age. Old letters
to a friend, a caterpillar house, my dads old sweater.

I breathe in the remaining scents in that sweater, hoping for
anything familiar. But the years have replaced his scent, which
I catch on the wind every now and then.

I put everything away, carefully tucked into their boxes, and fold
the cardboard lids into place.

I feel nostalgic, loved, fulfilled in that old wooden room, and
close the door littered with stickers from my life.

3 WORDS

I got you. Those 3 little words have become our family's mantra. It's something I've said to Paige since she was little, a reassuring phrase most parents say to their children. One day it became more. I can't pinpoint exactly when, but the phrase transformed into something stronger, something with weight.

I got you. It's our mantra for everything now. It's my reassurance to my daughter. She knows when I say that, nothing bad will happen. I'm there. She won't fall, she won't get hurt, and I'll make everything better. I say it when she's scared, hurt, tired, and it isn't just words. It's a promise. It has substance in our family. I'm here, and no matter what happens, I'm not leaving.

I got you. It's the rock of our relationship. When shit gets hard, those three simple words are all we need to hear. Living apart over half of the month gets hard. It doesn't matter how long you've been doing it, it doesn't get easier. There are times where we just simply miss each other. Insecurities can run rampant, the mind can wander to dark places. Those three simple words bring us back into the light. It showers us with strength and resolve. It straightens our shoulders, squares our stance. It heightens our focus and expands our heart. Those words go to the soul. It's our promise. No matter what. I've got you. It's us. Always.

C L A Y

Once upon a time I was malleable,

Soft to the touch.

But time has hardened me.

Left out in the sun too long,

I've become rough, sharp.

Cracks have started to form,

Yet I've become strong.

What once would have washed away with the rain

now stands strong in the storm.

I stand upright these days,

Before, I folded easily upon myself.

I once was a hobby,

Tossed around by unskilled hands.

But time has hardened me,

And now I draw blood.

INSANITY

A mind fractured

A crevasse in an iceberg

Screaming and moaning as it's joints dislocate

Pieces of thought that once made sense.

Like magnetic words on a refrigerator

Fallen to the ground

Rearranged in senseless sentences.

Synapses reach across the divide

Trying to make a connection.

Drowning in toxins,

Floating to the surface like goldfish in a bowl.

The stench of death

Decaying dreams,

Necrotic thoughts.

An alcoholic mind.

An insane mind.

MY FATHER'S MOTHER

My fathers mother keeps secrets in her smile.

Wisdom flows from her fingers when she writes her dreams.

She has lines that hug her eyes when she smiles.

Her hair frames her beautiful face with gentle silver fingers

that brush her cheeks.

Words come from her lips without question,

She carries a lifetime on slender shoulders freckled with

days of sunshine.

Her eyes speak of pain but her laughter quickly brushes away

the footprints left by heartbreak.

She is the effect of lightning hitting sand,

A beautiful hardened thing that sparkles when it hits the light.

She is me, decades ago, formed by wind and rain,

strengthened by sun.

Her experiences reverberate in the hollow of my soul.

Memories of a prior life bouncing around in the present.

We are the same, separated only by time.

Living parallel lives across the strands of existence.

My fathers mother is my grandmothers granddaughter,

one and the same.

SETTING YOU FREE

Goodbye, sweet thing,
Your broken wings are healed.
I'd keep you forever, safe with me,
But you are not mine.
You belong in the trees,
Skimming the pond with the tips of a feather.
You are of the wild,
The untamed.
I sense some of me in you,
The rebellious blood flowing in your veins.
The need to soar,
Free from the bonds of the heart.
As I open my hands,
Holding you one last time,
I hope you'll look back as you fly away.
But you don't.
You don't belong to me,
I'm not sure you ever did.
Thank you for letting me love you for a little while.
Goodbye sweet thing,
Your broken wings are healed now.

ONCE UPON A TIME

Life sprawled out before us,

An endless red carpet of possibilities.

Magic was real,

Love, unconditional.

Our feet hitting pavement,

Effortless propulsion.

Heroes put us on their shoulders,

Lifted us over waves.

Responsibility just a thought, far ahead,

Dancing in the heat above the asphalt.

Monsters only lived under the bed.

Once upon a time,

We were untouched.

Like dew delicately perched on blades of grass,

We stood on the precipice of sunrise.

Wavering between realms of childhood and reality.

Once upon a time.

DOT DOT DOT

Why can't you just…

Why don't you just…

You're just so…

Three dots.

An infamy of not good enoughs

Hang in the air like cigarette smoke.

Swirling around me

Turning my stomach.

Long after it fades from sight

I recognize its scent

Soaked into my pores.

Reminding me of imperfection

The constant grasping

At the edges

Of good enough.

HOLE IN THE GROUND

We buried ourselves

So deep in that hole

Wading in darkness

Just two tortured souls.

Years I'd been down there

In the muck and the dark

Knowing love and pain

Unable to tell them apart.

One day I woke up

Shoulder deep in the mud,

I looked around disgusted

At what I'd allowed to be done.

I made a break for it

Clawed my way to the edge,

Trying to escape

While you grasped at my legs.

You wrestled me down

Several times while I climbed

Desperate for freedom

And a rational mind.

I knew I had to put distance

Between me and your fists

Even though the call to return

Was difficult to resist.

The fear of the unknown

Was more than I thought

Instead of you, it was my mind

That had to be fought.

The temptation to go back

Even though I knew was insane

Just went to show

The disease in my brain.

Somehow I stayed free

And never turned around

Now I enjoy the sun

And the peace that I've found.

I doubt you've found light

You probably just enjoy the sound

Of your own voice echoing

From that hole in the ground.

SILENCE

I stand quietly in the silence of my mind.
This space used to be so loud.
Here I can stand tall,
Confident and unafraid.
Locked away inside of myself,
A place that used to be a prison,
Now is the last of my defenses.
I run here to hide,
Away from the second guesses,
The not good enoughs.
It's quiet here,
I can hear myself think.
The outside world is so loud,
So full of hate.
People speak only to make noise.
Here, in my mind,
The silence knows me.
I am a warrior.
I display my scars proudly,
I flex my muscles,
I am confident of my worth.
Out there, I'm not so sure.
But here, I know who I am.

M O M

You spoke her name quietly,
Whispering it to hold her near.
Fondly telling stories,
Reminiscence you hold dear.
Times of dancing around the living room,
And the records she would play.
Leaving out the parts of empty bottles,
The flashing lights in the driveway.

You entered motherhood
A lot differently than me.
Your toolbox was missing so many things,
So many memories.
We are what our mothers teach us,
They mold us with their soul.
Sometimes though, their demons
Are more than they can control.

These things are often passed down
From generations on,
Unless a strong one stops it
From continuing beyond.
You took this duty upon yourself,
A warrior standing tall,
A guardian before her children
Promising to end it all.

You had nothing more
Than a memory and a plan
A promise to your children
To do everything you can.
You ended what began
Generations ago,
And began a new tradition
Where only love would show.

FATHERS

He traded my innocence for double vision,

Bargained away my childhood for relief from his.

Infiltrated every happy memory with stumbling and slurring.

Learning to drive was just a DD in disguise.

He made me think it was all normal,

Infusing dysfunction in my core.

Then he passed me the bottle,

And left me with a decade long hangover.

They say women search for men like their fathers.

FOREVER 3

I find myself floating back to the place in my mind where I keep
her memories.

I still haven't taught myself to leave that door open, allowing
them to come and go as they please.

They aren't just photos and movies, but a recreation of real life,
full of emotions. Acting themselves out in front of me.

I've frozen her in time. Three years wrapped up in a bow.

I keep them all in that back room in my mind. Revisiting it to
hold her stuffed animals close, breathe in the remaining smell of
her, or run my hands through old records of her voice.

Projecting home movies on an old white sheet, she comes alive
just like I remember her. Singing ABCs and reciting colors.

Her voice has changed now, and with it, the tone. But to me
she will always be three, singing "I've got sunshine" with a half
naked Barbie.

RETROSPECTION

We all can remember a time when things were easy.
When things made sense, when breathing didn't take effort.
When you didn't need to pause and quiet your thoughts,
to steady your heart.

Some look back on this time fondly. Some miss the way things
were. Some claw their insides trying to rid themselves of the
blackness that set in, the venom that coagulated their thoughts
somewhere along the way.

The need to viscerally rip open your body, to bleed out the toxins
that seem to settle into your very bones, is so painfully real.
Ripping yourself open in hopes that by shining sunlight inside
something green will grow from that infected soil.

Decades were spent attaching leeches to my skin, bloodletting
to remove the darkness from within me. I don't think I'll ever
get a chance to experience the freedom that I once felt before
the darkness consumed me, but the light is finally getting in.
I don't know where the darkness went. I don't know how it got
out…but the sunlight that took its place is finally starting to
help something grow.

PAIGE

I worried I wouldn't love you as much as the one I lost. She held the majority of my heart hostage.

Her smile, her laugh, the way her hair curled after a bath took up all corners of my soul.

I worried there would be no way you could compete with the love and loss that consumed me.

Then you came. In 2 minutes you came.

You looked at me and the hostage situation ended.

She had not left, just simply moved over to make room. The loss lessened, the pain softened.

You healed wounds that were so deep with a blink of your beautiful brown eyes. Your light, your laugh, the way you master things with such ferocity.

You were born with the strength of a warrior, a survivor who had no idea what she had fought through.

You destroyed the questions and worry your mother had and came into the world ready to conquer it all. Conquer my heart.

You are the light. The happiness. The perfection. It will never be tainted.

ONE PLUS ONE

One plus one equals two. That's what they tell you in school.
If you work hard, and are a good person, then good things will
happen.

What happens when you work hard, and you're an amazing
person, yet bad things happen? One plus one equals forty eight.

When you were little, you had dreams and plans for the future.
You had sticks and fuzzy sweaters, a blanket and your mommy.
Everything was safe, back then one plus one equaled two.

The math changes, exponentials and imaginary numbers come
into play. One plus one isn't an easy equation anymore.

You would have never guessed what you ended up being, snug-
gled up in your crib, life and endless possibilities ahead of you.

You ended up being an amazing person who worked hard. You
ended up being a father, brother, son. But it ended.

One plus one didn't end up equaling two.

THE NIGHT WE SAID GOODBYE

I sat in the backseat as we weaved our way through the back
roads of Oak View. I stared out the window, not one word
spoken. I don't remember who was in the car or even what time
it was, I just remember every mile away from you.

The hours have become blank to me, a mental street sweep
of debris. That night I didn't know how I would fall asleep.
Everything and nothing filled the spots of my mind that still
functioned.

Then the noise began. Quietly, knuckles rapped on the wood
table at the end of the hallway that sat right outside my
childhood bedroom door. Every time I picked my head up off
the pillow, they stopped. I laid my head down again, the knuckles
drummed the wood. I picked my head up and laid it back down
quickly, praying the drumming continued. The drumming
somehow put me immediately to sleep.

I awoke in the morning trying to come up with a logical
explanation of the noise and finding none. I know you were there
drumming your giant strong fingers against the table like you
had all my life. I always tried to match that drumming, laughing
when my tiny fingers would make tiny noises and get sore.

It was a fitting goodbye. An inside joke only we would know.

18

My grief is 18 today.
An adult.
At first it was wobbly and needed constant attention.
It took up so much of my time, looking after it, tending to it.
Then it learned to move, and I chased it everywhere.
I fed it and taught it, listened to it and fought with it.
We went everywhere together, hand in hand.
Those teenage years were the hardest, it tested me over and over.
Then my grief's mother came into my life and spoke to it.
She stroked its hair, whispered in its ear and cradled it close.
My grief sighed, lowered its shoulders and leaned into her,
so content that she was there.
She took my grief during its most troubling teenage years
and tamed it.
Now it is 18. An adult.
Full fledged and ready to leave the nest.

GRANNY'S SHOES

My favorite pair of shoes were worn by the woman who carried
the world on her shoulders.
That pair of leather flip flops with etching on the straps
were as perfect as the woman who would become my best friend.
Her impeccably styled hair, stylish peach sweater and
perfectly unwrinkled white capris were only outshone by
the sun on the beach that day. Her oversized sunglasses
sat on her beautiful face, somehow untouched
by the years of worry, damage and tears.
She herded five grandchildren across the sand that day,
laughing and taking photographs with her film camera.
She tried her hardest to cover up the distance
with ice cream and smiles, but her heart ache showed through.
My favorite pair of shoes were worn by the woman
who carried guilt and sadness. The woman who fought on
despite what was stacked against her. The woman who never asked
for a prince to save her, she wielded her sword
against the mightiest dragon, and never faltered.
My favorite pair of shoes were worn by the strongest woman
I've ever met in my life.

PINK CLOUD

I thought sobriety was like a light switch.
You flipped it on, and light flooded the room. Angels sang,
blessings rained down from above, everything fell into place
and there were no more missing puzzle pieces.
I thought it would feel like I had my own personal theme song
playing in the background, like a lead character strutting down
the street in some bad ass action movie.
I thought everything would make sense and nothing would be
hard anymore. The veil would be lifted and my sight restored.
The pink cloud.
Sobriety is more like being color blind. Hearing people say the
world has more to it, but not quite knowing what it is. Then
someone buys you the fancy pair of glasses that let you see color.
You put them on and are amazed at how vibrant the world is,
how clear and bright it seems.
It's the same world though. Same shit. Just prettier.

POSTPARTUM

I didn't notice the sky getting darker,
The clouds creeping in, quietly blotting out the sun.
If it had been sudden I may have looked up, looking for what
had changed. Then my world darkened,
Familiarity caused dread in my heart.
It was back.
I hadn't expected it for another few months, but here it was early.
The darkness.
Postpartum.
5 months pregnant is not what one would associate with
postpartum, but here I was.
3 years prior I had felt those fingers piercing my skull.
For months I felt it inside my head, pushing and pulling my
thoughts in wild directions.
Now without warning I can feel it behind me, waiting.
The skies have already darkened, the shadow impending.
Here I sit helpless, waiting for those cold fingers to touch me
once again.

4TH OF JULY

One of my dad's favorite holidays was the 4th of July. Any
holiday that is celebrated by bbqing for mass amounts of people
was guaranteed to make his top 3. Add in explosives, family time
and warm weather, you had a winner.

He loved spending way too much money on fireworks and when
I'd remind him that it was against the law, he'd giggle, stick his
middle finger in the air towards the street and blow a raspberry
while grabbing his butt cheek. Typical dad response. We never
got caught, but I guarantee if we ever had, the police officer
would have ended up staying for burgers.

You couldn't help but love my dad, he was infectious. Not just
his personality, but all of him. His entire existence made you
want to be near him. He was a walking magnet of happiness
and safety. A warm place to land and somewhere you knew food
would be readily served no matter the time.

Summer was his favorite. He'd go barefoot, pulling out the
charcoal and the old Weber. Burgers were his specialty, he could
tell you the internal temp of a burger by glancing at the bbq
even after a 12 pack or two. He'd stand next to that damn bbq
for hours, assuming the alpha male role and grunting at the fire.

I was always afraid of fireworks. I have no idea why. Nothing
traumatic ever happened, I just hated them being next to me.
Enter my father's hilariously sick sense of humor. He'd chase
me with sparklers while I screamed until I cried, usually with
him unable to breathe from laughing so hard. He was always the
prankster.

This time of year just feels like him. It's fitting he left us during the summer. Sitting outside near his bbq, barefoot and enjoying the fading warmth of the day. I hope he was looking forward to the 4th. Planning in his head the feast he'd make for all those who would come to share the day.

TODAY'S NEWS

My heart is heavy
The screaming is so loud.
I feel the weight of the world,
The hatred, the pain, the death
It's tangible.
I taste it, I hear it, I feel it.
It echoes, reverberating between my ribs
Squeezing my heart
Stifling my breath.
The world is clutching itself,
Writhing on the ground
A man covered with a million biting ants.
It hurts to breathe,
Every inhale is toxic,
Burning violence slicing my lungs.
My heartbeat feels uneven,
Anxiety squeezes my insides
A tight fist around a toothpaste tube.
Talking heads on a screen
Yell into the void,
Interrupting each other
With gunfire and good hair.
Words traipse across the screen,
Scrawling warnings,
And the weather.

HOMELESSNESS

I saw a life overturned on the highway today,
Dreams and hopes scattered across the lanes
Blowing in the wind as a woman ran to catch them.
Backed up for miles we crept along,
Not one person stopping in the procession,
Staring at the woman collecting her things.
Her children caught our gaze, tears in their eyes,
watching memories flutter down the asphalt.
A future rolled under our tires, but we didn't slow down.
Moments later the accident faded from thought
and the procession went about its way,
Focused on to-do lists and errands.
While the children watch their mother chase belongings
on the breeze, hoping she returns.

SADNESS

Your embrace, in the beginning, cold

Became warm with your ever persisting presence.

My lover, my constant companion.

Forever in the shadows,

Waiting for happiness to turn its back

Then our tryst continues.

How beautiful you are, serene sadness.

Full emotion pouring from inside.

A deeper feeling than I've ever experienced.

The ache of loss, pure unbridled sorrow.

How sweet the experience of exposing your soul,

Bleeding it out through your eyes.

There is no truer form

Than sadness

ALBUQUERQUE

I took a left at Albuquerque
You kept straight on the road.
Heading to the bright lights of Vegas
And the promises of hookers and blow.

I headed left for salvation
The pulpit, the pew and the priest,
You had a date with the devil
And that whiskey neat.

You rolled your eyes
Slammed gears
Squealed the tires
Leaving dirt in my teeth
And tears in my eyes.

I took a left at Albuquerque
You kept straight on the road.
I turned left for salvation
You kept straight for hookers and blow.

I took comfort in that back room
The stench of ashtrays and hope
One hand on the good book
Silence stuck in my throat.

They promised salvation
One day at a time.
While you pulled in to Vegas
Pupils blown, feeling fine.

Now I'm stepping my way
Through humility and hope
While you're cradling you're whiskey
Your hookers and dope.

NARCISSUS

Little girl watch out
For sweet narcissus
That beautiful thing
Has a poisonous existence

It's perfume will convince you
That you're fucked in the head
And you'll tear yourself apart
While you swallow the meds

The enticing bloom
Hypnotizes your brain
Swearing you're crazy
Certifiably insane

Narcissus is perfect
Beautiful and complete
You, poor child
Could never compete

Surrender yourself
Your sword and you soul
Admit your inferiority
While he swallows you whole.

You'll never be the same
After picking this flower
It doesn't covet your wealth
It's your worth it devours.

CLOSURE

I dialed that number,
Shaking inside.
I tried to speak with strength,
But the fear could not hide.
You noticed the quiver
And you jumped on the chance
To relive your manipulations
And continue the dance.
I spoke in circles
Trying to get closure,
Convincing myself
That the trauma was over.
But you are still you
Righteous and bold
Then I noticed something off,
Your voice sounded old
You'd become tired and broken
Noticing cracks in the slab
Not as strong anymore
More regretful and sad.
Your voice no longer scared me,
Like it did way back then.
Back when you'd destroy me
Over and over again
You left scars deep within me
That are present today.
To me it was life changing,
To you, it was Wednesday.
After I hung up the phone,
I breathed a sigh of relief
Because the terror you caused
The scars that formed so deep,
They've lessened in color
And the pain, not so strong,
Because of a man who loves me
The man I deserved all along.

IMPOSTER

She used to be my hero. A strong tiny woman, fiercely defending her family. Hell came on the heels of that woman. She loved as hard as she hated, and both were forces to be reckoned with.

Behind the facade, behind the strength, the love, was something else. Addiction. Judging. Manipulation. Vindictive malice.

How do you love someone who has been so evil to those you love. Someone who has been so evil to you? Somehow, I did. My heart feels guilty, she has done so much damage, but I have such fond memories of her. Memories of the past, at war with my knowledge of now.

Loving her is like loving a wild animal. You know you'll get bit sometime in your life, but you take the risk and love it anyways. When it draws blood you chalk it up, that's just what it is. Unpredictable. Wild. Incapable of human emotions.

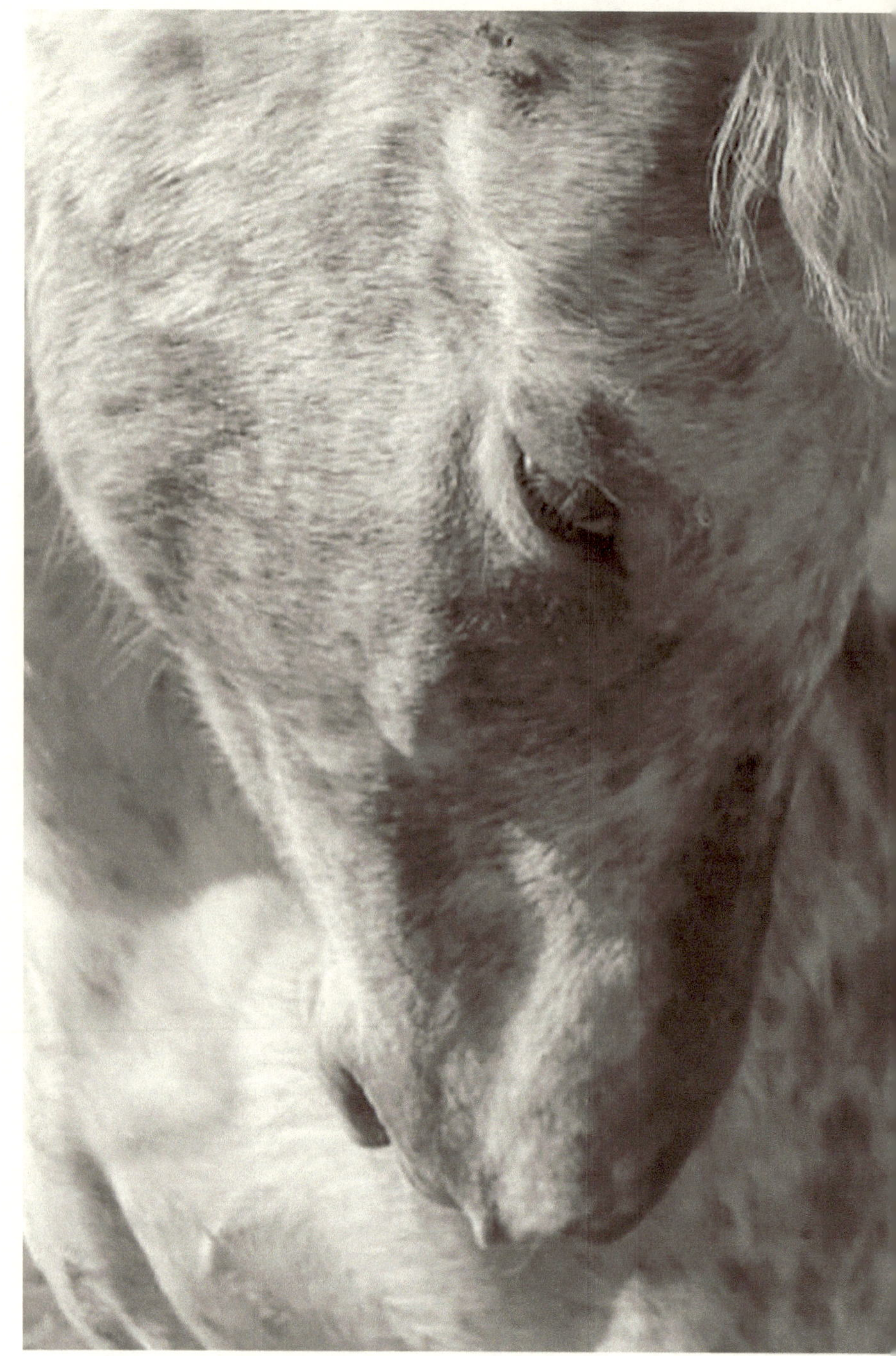

SWEET BOY

When you were sent from the heavens,
The Lord gave you no bounds.
You were born from the stars,
Bearing their crowns.

He knew you were different,
Not one to follow the herd.
So he bestowed upon you something special,
Something only you deserved.

He placed the sea in your eyes,
Planted your feet on the ground,
Lit a fire in your heart,
And lifted your head to the clouds.

He gifted me you,
With a 700-year-old soul.
Teaching me lessons,
Of things you could never know.

He told me you were a dreamer,
A doer, a thinker.
A moonlight watcher,
A magic bringer.

THE LAST BABY

I cried today.
My friend is having a baby
A little girl, just like you.
I dug into saved bags of clothes
Little living doll outfits
Full of pink bows and flowers,
Whales and kittens.
I put them to my face,
Breathed in the remaining smells
Newness, milk and warm skin.
I folded those little pieces,
Patting each one as I stacked them
Higher and higher in that gift bag.
I remembered every laugh, every cry
 Every cuddle I gave you in each one.
I couldn't give away my favorites,
I returned those to that box in the closet,
Never to be worn again.
It's fitting that you're the last,
The one who needs me the most.
The longest one to breastfeed,
The one who has never seen me drunk.
The final chapter of my newborns,
The one I finally did it right.
As you grow I'll go back,
Touch those little trinkets,
Breathe in the remaining smells,
Of my last baby.

LITTLE HANDS

Little hands
Reach inside of me
Fixing old wounds
From long before them.
Little giggles heal broken pieces
Pulling my heart strings
Together like stitches.
Little smiles all knowing,
Secrets from other worlds.
Little feet leave impressions
Tracing the path
Through parallels of sanity.
Little eyes make bubbles in my soul
Carried upwards
Bursting in my eyes
Overflowing into my smile.
Little ones
Stitching me together
With strands of innocence.

I DON'T LIVE THERE ANYMORE

I visit that place often
That home I used to know
Littered with broken bottles
And empty baggies of blow.

Although I no longer live there
I can't help but venture back
To visit the ghosts that haunt me
And watch the movies of my past.

The movies play in front of me
Vivid visions of the old me
Stumbling and lying
A mother in make believe.

I live somewhere new now
With unbroken promises and hope
A place that's no longer littered
With whiskey bottles and dope.

I visit that place often
That home I just can't sell
The dark hole where I hit bottom
Of my childhood wishing well.

IN APPRECIATION

Thank you to my Granny for the gift of generational sobriety.
Who knew when you stepped in that room so many decades
ago, the gift you would be bestowing upon your granddaughter?

Thank you to my husband for unwavering support, and many
hours wrangling children while I tapped away at my keyboard.

Thank you to my mother for listening to poem after poem,
no matter how dark or difficult to hear.

Thank you to my children for stitching me back together when
my stuffing came loose.

Thank you to my sobriety tribe. You know who you are.